W9-AGC-877

NASCAR RACING

Racing with the
Pit Crew

by A. R. Schaefer

Consultant:
Betty L. Carlan
Research Librarian
International Motorsports Hall of Fame
Talladega, Alabama

Capstone
press
Mankato, Minnesota

Edge Books are published by Capstone Press,
151 Good Counsel Drive, P.O. Box 669, Mankato, Minnesota 56002.
www.capstonepress.com

Library of Congress Cataloging-in-Publication Data
Schaefer, A. R. (Adam Richard), 1976–
    Racing with the pit crew / by A.R. Schaefer.
    p. cm.—(Edge Books NASCAR racing)
    Includes bibliographical references and index.
    ISBN 0-7368-3776-0 (hardcover)
    1. Pit crew—Juvenile literature. 2. Automobile racing—Juvenile literature. I. Title.
II. Series.
GV1029.13.S35 2005
796.72—dc22   2004013900

Summary: Covers what each member of a NASCAR pit crew does during pit stops,
    including training and pit stop strategy.

Editorial Credits
Tom Adamson, editor; Jason Knudson, set designer; Enoch Peterson, book designer;
    Jo Miller, photo researcher; Scott Thoms, photo editor

Photo Credits
AP/Wide World Photos/Steve Helber, 25
Corbis/Reuters/Doug Murray, 14; NewSport/George Tiedemann, 28–29
Getty Images Inc./Craig Jones, cover, 27; Rusty Jarrett, 9; Darrell Ingham, 21;
    Todd Warshaw, 29
Navy Photo by J01 Mark Rankin, 11; PH2 Brett Dawson, 19
Sam Sharpe, 5, 6, 7, 10, 12, 13, 23, 24
WireImage/Brian A. Westerholt, 17

1 2 3 4 5 6 10 09 08 07 06 05

Table of Contents

CHAPTER 1

The Pit Stop

A race car roars down pit road. The pit crew gets ready for action. Everyone grabs their tools. When the car gets close, all seven workers jump over the wall.

Once the car stops, the jackman slides the jack under the right side of the car. With one pump, the two right side tires are off the ground. The tire changers use airguns to loosen the lugnuts. They whip off the old tires. The tire carriers push new tires in place. In a second, the tire changers have lugnuts tightened on the new tires. The jackman releases the jack. Everyone runs to the other side of the car to change the left side tires.

The pit crew gets to work before the race car even stops.

Learn about:

➜ Changing tires

➜ Fueling up

➜ The pit crew

At the same time, the gasman fills the car's 22-gallon (83-liter) fuel cell. The catch can man catches the overflow. When the tank is full, the catch can man raises his hand.

The jackman drops the jack. The car takes off with the tires smoking. The entire stop took less than 15 seconds.

The tire changers and tire carriers have to hurry around the car.

The catch can man signals to the driver when the fuel cell is full.

NASCAR Pit Crews

In NASCAR racing, the drivers are in the spotlight. But the driver is part of a team. Some team members work on the car in the shop. Some work on it in the garage at the racetrack. Other people work on the car in the pit during the race. They are called the pit crew. Pit crews must work fast. Each second that a car is in the pit box is a second that it's not racing.

CHAPTER 2

Inside the Pit

Seven workers jump over the wall to work on a car during a normal NASCAR pit stop. Each worker has only one or two jobs. Speed and safety are the two main goals of pit workers.

The crew chief is in charge of the pit crew. He makes decisions about what to do during a pit stop. He uses a radio to talk with the driver. The crew chief decides if the car needs any adjustments.

Tires

Five members of the pit crew change the tires. The jackman uses a hydraulic jack to lift one side of the car. When one side is off the ground, two tires can be taken off. After the two tires are changed, the jackman hurries around the car to lift the other side.

The jackman lifts the car so the tires can be changed.

Learn about:

→ The crew chief

→ What the pit crew does

→ Pit road dangers

The pit crew has two tire changers. One person changes the front tires, and the other changes the rear tires. The tire changers use an airgun to loosen and tighten the lugnuts. The tire changers' job is to get the tires off and on as fast as they can.

The tire changers need to loosen and tighten five lugnuts on each tire.

The tire changers work fast to get their driver back on the track right away.

The two tire carriers help the tire changers. The tire carriers don't use any tools during a pit stop. Their job is to take new tires from behind the wall and put them on the car for the tire changers.

"Pit crewmen are amazing athletes with special talent . . . but go totally unnoticed unless they screw up."
—Marty Smith, nascar.com column writer, 8-29-03

The gasman and catch can man fill the fuel cell in a matter of seconds.

Fuel

While five crew members work on the tires, two others are making sure the car is full of fuel. The gasman fills the fuel cell. The gasman uses one or two gas cans on a pit stop, depending on how empty the fuel cell is.

The catch can man catches fuel when the tank is full. The catch can is shaped like a box. It has a valve that plugs in to the back of the car. When the tank is full, the extra fuel comes out the valve and into the catch can. The catch can man then raises his hand to signal the driver that the fuel cell is full.

The Spotter

An important member of a race team who doesn't work in the pit area is the spotter. The spotter watches the race from high above the track. He talks to the driver by radio. The spotter tells the driver what's happening on the track. If a spotter sees a wreck, he tells the driver how to avoid it. The spotter also tells the driver where to pass another car.

Spotters watch the race from high above the track.

The pit area can be dangerous.

Safety

The pit area can be a dangerous place. Equipment is heavy and dangerous. Crew members run in front of the race car while it's still moving. The crew has to trust the driver to be careful.

Fuel can catch on fire. Crew members wear firesuits. The firesuits are hot and heavy, but they protect against fire. Each pit also has fire extinguishers.

NASCAR has rules to protect crew members. Drivers must obey a speed limit on pit road. Drivers are not allowed to pass on pit road. Crew members must enter the pit box only when the car is two pit boxes away. Since 2002, crew members have been required to wear helmets.

"It [the helmet] saved my life. I mean, I'm bruised and all that—but at least my eggs ain't scrambled."
—Shawn Pincola, tire carrier, after being hit by a race car in the pit box, nascar.com, 4-11-02

CHAPTER 3

Pit Crew Training

All members of a pit crew must be quick and strong. Pit crew members haul heavy equipment around in a small space. The jack weighs about 35 pounds (16 kilograms). The jackman has to run with it to both sides of the race car. The gasman lifts a gas can that weighs about 80 pounds (36 kilograms) when it's full. Tires weigh about 75 pounds (34 kilograms) each. Many pit crew members lift weights to have good upper body strength.

The gasman has to be able to lift the heavy gas can and get it into place quickly.

Learn about:

→ **Heavy equipment**

→ **Practice**

→ **Careful planning**

Pit Practice

To have a perfect pit stop, each movement needs to be done a certain way. The crew practices often. With heavy equipment and a small work area, they must know exactly what to do and when.

Most teams have a practice area. A driver pulls the car in to a practice pit box, and the crew acts like it's a normal pit stop.

Sometimes these practice stops are videotaped. Later, the crew watches the tape. The crew chief helps the team improve its performance. He might tell one member to watch out for an air hose or tell another person to stand in a different place at the beginning of the pit stop. Even small movements of crew members can save time during a pit stop.

"The crew won the race—not me. I just did my part by driving. They got me in position on that stop toward the end."
—Tony Stewart, 7-24-03, nascar.com

The crew's every movement during a stop is carefully planned.

Tire changers practice with a cardboard cutout of a wheel. They put a marker on the end of an airgun. They practice putting the marker onto the cutout like they would put the airgun on the lugnuts of a wheel. These exercises are timed with a stopwatch. The goal is to do a perfect job as fast as possible.

Most training takes place during the off-season. During the racing season, the crews are too busy traveling around the country to spend much time practicing. They practice only if there is a major problem.

The race team gets the tires ready before the race starts.

CHAPTER 4

Beyond Tires and Fuel

During a race, a pit crew works a total of only one or two minutes. Those minutes are very important. Many races are won or lost because of pit stops.

First Laps

After the first few laps, the crew chief wants to know how the car is handling. He talks with the driver on the radio. He asks the driver if the car is too loose or too tight. If the driver says it's too loose, he's in danger of losing control in the corners. A car that's too tight is hard to turn.

If the car is running well, the crew prepares for a normal pit stop. The first pit stop comes when the car is close to running out of fuel. If there is a caution for a wreck or other problem, the driver may stop sooner. A regular pit stop includes changing all four tires and filling the fuel cell. The crew may make minor adjustments to the car so it handles better.

When everyone pits at the same time, pit road looks chaotic.

Learn about:

→ A typical pit stop

→ Windshield tear-offs

→ Gas-and-go stops

During some stops, a crew member pulls off a windshield tear-off sheet.

Special Stops

Stock car windshields have tear-off sheets. A tear-off sheet is a thin piece of plastic over the windshield. Using tear-off sheets is much faster than cleaning the windshield. One of the crew members pulls off the sheet with a free hand. A car usually has three tear-off sheets for a race.

If a car has been bumped or has scraped the wall, it might be damaged. The crew might have to pound the car with a hammer to make it the right shape. The crew members try to keep the car as aerodynamic as possible, even with damage. They also try to keep bent fenders from rubbing against the tires. They may use duct tape to repair a damaged fender.

The crew repairs a damaged fender during a stop.

Other Pit Stops

Sometimes, the driver comes in to the pit for a gas-and-go. During a gas-and-go, the driver only comes in for fuel. No tires are changed. These stops save several seconds. Gas-and-go stops are usually used only near the end of a race. They're used when the car might run out of fuel before the last lap.

The driver may come in for a two-tire pit stop. The crew changes only two tires and fills the fuel cell. On most racetracks, the right side tires wear down faster than the left tires. Having two new right side tires can give the car an advantage for a few laps.

"Our biggest problem this year has been these dumb pit stops. It's been horrible. Instead of having 13-second stops, we've been having 17s and 18s and 19s."
—Rusty Wallace, 3-23-03, nascar.com

Being part of a NASCAR pit crew is exciting and fast-paced. With a fast pit stop, the driver can move up in track position. The crew might end up celebrating with the driver in the winner's circle.

The whole team enjoys winning.

1. Jackman
2. Rear tire carrier
3. Rear tire changer
4. Front tire carrier
5. Front tire changer
6. Catch can man
7. Gasman

Glossary

aerodynamic (air-oh-dye-NAM-mik)—designed to reduce air resistance

caution (KAW-shun)—a time during a race when drivers have to slow down and are not allowed to pass; a caution occurs after a crash or when the track crew has to clean up debris.

fuel cell (FYOO-uhl SELL)—the fuel tank in race cars

hydraulic (hye-DRAW-lik)—something that works on power created by liquid being forced under pressure through pipes

lugnut (LUHG-nuht)—a small piece of equipment that fastens a tire to the wheel hub

pit box (PIT BOKS)—the area a race car must be in during a pit stop

valve (VALV)—a movable part that controls the flow of liquid or gas through a pipe

Read More

Barber, Phil. *From Finish to Start: A Week in the Life of a NASCAR Racing Team.* The World of NASCAR. Maple Plain, Minn.: Tradition Books, 2004.

Buckley, James Jr. *Life in the Pits: Twenty Seconds That Make the Difference.* The World of NASCAR. Excelsior, Minn.: Tradition Books, 2003.

Burt, William M. *Behind the Scenes of NASCAR Racing.* St. Paul, Minn.: Motorbooks International, 2003.

Internet Sites

FactHound offers a safe, fun way to find Internet sites related to this book. All of the sites on FactHound have been researched by our staff.

Here's how:

1. Visit *www.facthound.com*

2. Type in this special code **0736837760** for age-appropriate sites. Or enter a search word related to this book for a more general search.

3. Click on the **Fetch It** button.

FactHound will fetch the best sites for you!

Index